IN FOCUS: NATIVE AMERICANS

PUEBLO

HISTORY AND CULTURE

MARK STEWART

Cavendish Square

Published in 2026 by Cavendish Square Publishing, LLC
2544 Clinton Street, Buffalo, NY 14224

Website: cavendishsq.com

Portions of this work were originally authored by Linda Buellis and published as *Pueblo* (Spotlight on Native Americans). All new material this edition authored by Mark Stewart.

Publisher: Katie Kawa
Book Design: Lisa Miley

Portions of this work were reviewed by: Donald A. Grinde, Jr., Professor of Transnational/American Studies at the State University of New York at Buffalo.

Photo Credits: Bob Petley/Color Cards/Author's Collection (4); Library of Congress (5*, 13 bottom*, 17*); Underwood & Underwood Publishers/Wikimedia Commons (6 top); Duncan Gilbert/Shutterstock.com (6 bottom); Joseph Sohn/Shutterstock.com (7); Chris Maddaloni/CQ-Roll Call Group/Getty Images (9); National Park Service (10*); John K. Hillers/New Mexico History Museum (11*); Robert Alexander/Getty Images (12); A&P Johnston/Library of Congress (13 top*); Carlisle Indian School Digital Resource Center (15); The Merriman Co./Library of Congress (16*, 18*); Conrad Dunkerson (19); John Cancalosi/Photolibrary/Getty Images (20); H.S. Poley (21*); Courtesy of Nora Naranjo-Morse (22 top); Chris Felver/Archive Photos/Getty Images (23 bottom); National Park Service/Wikimedia Commons (25); Wolfgang Kaehler/LightRocket/Getty Images (26); Cordelia Wilson (27*); Fairfax Media via Getty Images/Fairfax Media via Getty Images via Getty Images (28); Joseph Sohn/Shutterstock.com (29).

Cover images (clockwise from top): Author's Collection; Simeon Schwemberger*; A&P Johnston/Library of Congress*; Edward Curtis/Library of Congress*; Duncan Gilbert/Shutterstock.com; Nativestock.com/Marilyn Angel Wynn/The Image Bank/Getty Images.

*These images are in the public domain.

Cataloging-in-Publication Data
Names: Stewart, Mark, 1960 July 7-.
Title: Pueblo history and culture / Mark Stewart.
Description: Buffalo, NY : Cavendish Square Publishing, 2026. | Series: In focus: Native Americans | Includes glossary and index.
Identifiers: ISBN 9781502674821 (pbk.) | ISBN 9781502674838 (library bound) | ISBN 9781502674845 (ebook)
Subjects: LCSH: Pueblo Indians--Juvenile literature. | Pueblo Indians--Social life and customs--Juvenile literature. | Indians of North America--Juvenile literature. | Indigenous peoples--Social life and customs--Juvenile literature.
Classification: LCC E99.P9 S94 2026 | DDC 978.9004'974--dc23

CPSIA compliance information: Batch #CS26CSQ: For further information contact Cavendish Square Publishing LLC at 1-877-980-4450.
Printed in the United States of America

CONTENTS

ABOUT OUR GLOSSARY

In this book, there may be several words or terms you are reading for the first time, or words that are familiar but used in an unusual way. All of these words appear in **bold type** throughout the book and are defined on page 30.

I AM THE LAND

The North American Southwest, which includes the states of Arizona and New Mexico—as well as northern Mexico—can be a harsh, challenging environment. Native plants and animals are not available in great abundance; access to water is unpredictable. It is not a **hospitable** place for humans. And yet, for thousands of years, people have found ways to survive and thrive here by understanding how to coax the resources they need from the land around them. The Pueblo people learned from the successes and failures of those who came before them and, today, 20 Puebloan tribes call this part of the world home.

This photo of an extended Pueblo family from the early 1900s shows a home that has added ground-floor doors and windows.

The Pueblo people are descended from a great farming civilization that archaeologists call the Ancestral Puebloans. Many know them as the Anasazi. They occupied the region where Arizona, New Mexico, Colorado, and Utah meet—sometimes called the "four corners." Their roots go back nearly 2,000 years. Before the Ancestral Puebloans, other ancient cultures occupied the region for 10,000 years or more. They are among the first humans that traveled to North America from Asia during and after the **Ice Age**. When these people arrived, the environment was cool and moist, with large animals to hunt. As the climate became hot and dry, and the

◀ The village in Taos, New Mexico, is typical of traditional Pueblo architecture.

Ceremonial life has been a central theme in Pueblo culture for centuries.

large animals disappeared, humans adjusted. They learned how to manage water in ways that enabled them to grow crops so that they had a reliable source of food.

Pueblo ancestors were masters of their environment for many centuries. They built large, permanent structures that survive to this day. However, *they* did not survive. When times are good, populations tend to expand. When challenges arise, it can be difficult to "shrink" a population. Evidence of long periods of drought—coupled with conflicts with people migrating north from Mexico—suggest that the Ancestral Puebloans had no

choice but to abandon their cities between the years 1200 and 1400—and use their knowledge and skills to create other, smaller settlements.

The ancestors of the Pueblo people migrated south, where the environment was more forgiving. They settled near the Rio Grande and Zuni rivers in New Mexico and the Hopi mesas of Arizona and split into two cultural groups: the Western Pueblos and Eastern Pueblos. These groups divided further into distinct communities that developed different languages, but retained common agricultural techniques, religious beliefs, and **clan** and cultural traditions.

To call the Pueblos a single "tribe" would be incorrect. Indeed, the United States government officially recognizes 19 different Pueblo tribes in New Mexico alone. Other Pueblo communities are located in parts of Arizona and Texas. They speak several different languages, including Tewa, Tanoan, and Keres. All told, at least 75,000 Pueblo people live in the United States.

◀ Ancestral Puebloans built permanent settlements like this one in Mesa Verde National Park in Colorado.

FIRST CONTACT

In 1540, Spanish explorer Francisco Vázquez de Coronado set out from Mexico in search of gold. Moving north with 400 soldiers and more than 1,000 Native allies, the expedition encountered village after village that were home to large numbers of people. They called these people Pueblo, which is the Spanish word for "village" or "town." Decades of conflict, disease, and forced labor followed, killing thousands. Spanish **missionaries** tried to destroy the Pueblo religion—burning their places of worship and sacred objects—and convert the people to Christianity.

The Pueblo people learned quickly that opposition of any kind was met with extreme violence. In 1599, Spanish soldiers killed, **mutilated**, and enslaved more than 800 Acoma Pueblo men, women, and children. This attack was one of many that sparked a rebellion against the Spanish in 1680, organized by a religious leader named Po'Pay. It killed hundreds of soldiers and settlers,

This statue of Po'Pay, leader of the 1680 rebellion, is located in the Capitol building in Washington, D.C.

and drove more than 2,000 ranchers and farmers out of the region.

When the Spanish returned to Pueblo lands 12 years later, they treated the Pueblo people with more respect. However, incidents of brutality continued. An uneasy relationship followed until the 1800s, when Mexico declared independence from Spain and then the United States defeated Mexico in a war. In 1848, Pueblo lands fell under the control of the American government.

I AM A WARRIOR

The Pueblo Revolt of 1680 was one of most successful resistance movements in Native American history. Although the rebellion was rooted in anger and frustration, its success was not. The Pueblo people had a strong warrior tradition that was not only based on bravery and skill, but also communication. The concept of a warrior in Pueblo society placed a high value on concern and leadership for village members, organizing community defense, and involvement in the spiritual life.

This illustration of a Pueblo warrior shows a spear, shield, and bow and arrows.

Young men were trained in hand-to-hand combat with war clubs and tomahawks, as well as the use of the bow and arrow for hunting and

Potshuno, a famous Pueblo warrior, was also known for his great speed. It was said that he never lost a footrace against an American, Mexican, or Native American.

fighting. War clubs were made of hardwood with a stone attached to one end and a wrist strap at the other. They wielded these weapons with the skill of modern-day martial arts experts. Tomahawks served many purposes—including as tools and ceremonial items. Shields were also important in close combat.

Pueblo warriors also used spears very effectively. They relied on a device called an atlatl, which attached to the bottom of a spear and greatly increased its throwing distance and power. Village defense counted on walls and well-built homes. This strategy dated back to their ancestors, many of whom built settlements into cliff faces.

During the rebellion in 1680, Spanish settlers abandoned thousands of horses, which Pueblo warriors quickly adopted into their culture, adding mobility to their

fighting techniques. The same was true for firearms, which became more available in the 1700s.

Because the Pueblo people used the guns they acquired primarily for hunting, they became expert marksmen. In battles with Spanish, Mexican, and American settlers—who used guns mostly for protection—they were almost always better shots. Guns became an important **status symbol** for Pueblo warriors, who were almost exclusively men. Pueblo women, who were viewed as givers of life and not takers, rarely handled firearms of any kind.

After acquiring firearms, Pueblo hunters became expert marksmen. This gave them a great advantage in battle.

Prior to the arrival of the Spanish and the introduction of horses, warfare among the Pueblo people and their enemies was conducted on foot. Conflict was usually triggered by environmental conditions, like drought, which brought Native people into competition for resources.

A Zuni Pueblo boy holds a ceremonial shield and arrow during an annual gathering in Santa Fe, New Mexico.

A NEW REALITY

Pueblo lands came under United States control in the mid-1800s. This was the beginning of an era of ocean-to-ocean **expansion** for the nation, and the Pueblo people were directly in the path of this growth. Americans not only expected Pueblo people to learn English and practice Christianity, the government forced many of them from their tribal lands and onto reservations. Pueblo reservations were located in north-central New Mexico, from the area near Albuquerque up to Santa Fe and Taos, mostly near the Rio Grande.

This followed a brief period of independence and equality under Mexico, which regarded the Pueblo people as citizens. Their legal status now came under question: Were they U.S. citizens or were they "Indians"—and were their rights protected by U.S. law? This question lingered for decades.

Pueblo children were among the many thousands who were **compelled** to attend special boarding schools.

This "intake" photo from the Carlisle Indian School in Pennsylvania shows Pueblo children shortly after they arrived.

These schools were created in the 1870s and 1880s to strip Native Americans of their culture. Students were forbidden from speaking their Native languages, forced to wear school uniforms, and taught skills that the government believed would make them better Americans. Between school terms, Pueblo children were discouraged from returning home. Many were loaned out as cheap labor to nearby farms and factories.

BEING PUEBLO

Despite centuries of attempts to **diminish** their beliefs and traditions, the Pueblo people have shown a remarkable ability to preserve their culture. Part of that success has involved an openness to accepting new ideas. For example, many Pueblos practice a version of Christianity that blends with their long-held religious traditions and beliefs. During their three centuries under Spanish and Mexican rule, they were quick to adopt horses, cattle, and firearms, and cultivate new foods like apples, melons, tomatoes, peppers, and wheat.

A Pueblo boy plays in a plaza under the watchful eye of his family.

Pueblo bake ovens were an important part of village life.

Pueblo farmers added these crops to the corn, beans, squash, pumpkins, and sunflowers that were traditional parts of their diet. They gathered several varieties of nuts, collected roots, greens, and honey, and used salt to preserve meat. Although corn accounted for a huge percentage of the **calories** they consumed, the Pueblo people also hunted small game like gophers and rabbits, and larger animals, including deer and different types of antelope. Some villages also kept sheep and turkeys that they **domesticated**.

For hundreds of years, the rhythm of life in Pueblo villages has revolved around the living spaces they created. Traditional Pueblo architecture featured large, multi-level buildings that shared common walls and were arranged around a central plaza. Plazas were used for day-to-day work, social interaction, and ceremonies. Buildings did not have ground-level doors. A Pueblo home was entered by an exterior ladder, which could be pulled up in times of attack or danger. Today, Pueblo

villages have added a wide range of modern improvements (including front doors), while maintaining the historic style.

Pueblo villages include another ancient architectural feature, the kiva. A kiva is a large room—usually, but not always, round—that is located below ground level. It is a place of worship that is used for different spiritual ceremonies. Not surprisingly, kivas were a target of destruction for Spanish missionaries.

◀ This photo from the 1800s shows the network of ladders that were typical of Pueblo dwellings.

The symbolic importance of the kiva to Pueblo people is demonstrated by one of their most common origin stories. It says that their ancestors once lived underground and climbed out through a hole in the roof of the world below (in many stories using a ladder to do so). In another, their ancestors climbed through a hollow reed that was placed there by a being named Spider Grandmother. After arriving on Earth, the ancestors migrated and spread throughout the land.

SOMETHING SACRED

Pueblo spirituality and art have been connected for centuries. The best example is the kachina, a spiritual being that represents important aspects of Pueblo life, such as the sun, stars, corn, and different animals. There are more than 500 kachinas and, although they are not worshipped as gods, they possess great power.

Kachinas are represented in traditional ceremonies by men who wear kachina masks. The performer is said to have the kachina inside him when he participates in the ceremony. The Pueblo people also

Kachina dolls like this one were given to children to teach them about the world.

Maria Martinez, a legendary artist, helped to make Pueblo pottery famous throughout the world.

carve wooden dolls to represent kachinas. The dolls are given to Pueblo children as gifts and are used as a way to teach young people about the world, including how their ancestors survived and adapted to their environment. The care and well-being of a kachina is a great responsibility.

Pueblo pottery is considered one of the most highly developed Native American art forms. Potters make their works by hand-rolling long coils of clay and arranging them into the desired shape and size. They smooth the inside and outside, decorate it, and fire it to make it **durable** and waterproof. Pueblo pottery often features geometric designs with flower, animal, or bird patterns.

Juanita Suazo Dubray is a Taos Pueblo woman who became interested in Pueblo pottery in the 1980s.

Soon she became famous for her creations, which feature designs important to the Pueblo culture—such as **maize**, lizards, and turtles. Nora Naranjo-Morse, who works in a number of earth-based materials, specializes in large public art pieces.

"My work is influenced by the **arid** Southwestern environment, Pueblo culture and the rich Kha'p'o Owenge (Santa Clara Pueblo) community I have lived in all my life," she says.

The written word is also part of the Pueblo artistic tradition. During the 1960s and 1970s, a literary movement called the Native American Renaissance saw an explosion of creativity from writers and poets. Leslie Marmon Silko, a Laguna Pueblo woman, was part of that movement. She explored the relationship between the past and the present and how it impacted Pueblo life. Her most famous work, *Ceremony*, was celebrated for the importance it placed on Native American storytelling and traditions.

◀ Nora Naranjo-Morse displays a recent creation. Her work is inspired by the environment surrounding her community.

PAST, PRESENT, FUTURE

More than 75,000 people in the United States identify themselves as being Pueblo. They come from 21 federally recognized tribes, with all but two located in New Mexico. The New Mexico Pueblos are the Acoma, Cochiti, Isleta, Jemez, Laguna, Nambe, Ohkay Owingeh, Picuris, Pojoaque, Sandia, San Felipe, San Ildefonso, Santa Ana, Santa Clara, Santo Domingo, Taos, Tesuque, Zuni, and Zia. The Hopi, who are classified as a Pueblo people, live in Arizona, while the Ysleta del Sur live in Texas.

Although all Pueblo people trace their roots back to the same ancient population, they are not one "tribe" in the traditional sense. Their spiritual beliefs, traditions, and cultural mythology differ somewhat from group to group, and among them four different languages are spoken. Each has its own government and broad authority within its reservation.

Reservation economies depend on a combination of jobs, including agriculture and sales of crafts—including

Experts believe these rock carvings, located on Hopi land, represent the origin story of the ancient Puebloans. Hopis and Pueblos share the same ancestors.

pottery, jewelry, and other items that are highly prized among collectors. The town of Taos is one of America's oldest centers of art and artists. Starting in the 1890s, it began attracting some of the world's most creative painters, sculptors, and writers. They were drawn by the breathtaking scenery but also by the unique artistic style

Cordelia Wilson was one of the 20th century artists inspired by the landscape of Taos, New Mexico. This painting is entitled *Taos Mountain, Trail Home*.

and vision of the Pueblo people. Santa Fe also boasts a thriving artistic community.

The challenges that face all communities across America—including addiction, poverty and unemployment—impact Pueblo reservations as well. However, the uncertainty that comes with climate change may pose the greatest long-term threat. The Pueblo people live and work in a region where water has never been plentiful. Because their communities rely so heavily on agriculture, droughts have a great impact on their economy. So does the amount (and timing) of rain and

The Pueblo people preserve their culture in many ways, including wearing traditional clothing at public events.

snow. The result is smaller crop yields, which drive up costs for Pueblo ranchers. An effort is under way to create new policies that will help to inform and educate agricultural operations on tribal lands throughout the Southwest to prepare for, and respond to, drought and other effects of the changing climate.

One of the most important sources of income for the Pueblo people is tourism. Year in and year out, New Mexico is ranked among the top places in the world to visit. Pueblo communities have developed popular programs that promote their history and culture to the outside world, and generate millions of dollars annually. They also operate more than a dozen casinos. Income from these businesses and others go back into education, housing, and healthcare on the reservations.

◀ Pueblo ranchers and farmers are preparing to face the challenge of climate change in the future.

GLOSSARY AND FURTHER READING

GLOSSARY

Arid—Having almost no rain.

Calorie—A unit of energy used to calculate the nutritional value of foods.

Clan—A close-knit extended family related by kinship or common ancestors.

Compelled—Pressured or forced to do something.

Diminish—Make smaller or less important.

Domesticated—Tamed.

Durable—Able to withstand damage and wear.

Expansion—The process of becoming larger or more extensive.

Hospitable—Favorable for living.

Ice Age—A period marked by dropping global temperatures. The last Ice Age ended around 11,000 years ago.

Maize—Another name for corn.

Missionaries—People sent to promote Christianity to Native Americans by building religious outposts called missions.

Mutilated—Disfigured someone on purpose.

Status Symbol—A possession that shows off a person's wealth or influence.

BOOKS

Krupat, Arnold. *Boarding School Voices: Carlisle Indian School Students Speak*. Lincoln, NE: University of Nebraska Press, 2021.

Rossiter, Brienna. *The Trail of Tears*. Mendota Heights, MN: North Star Editions, 2025.

Tyler, Ron. *Native Americans: The Complete Plates of McKenney, Catlin, and Bodmer*. Cologne, Germany: Taschen America, 2024.

Various Authors. *My Life: Growing Up Native in America*. New York, NY: MTV Books/Simon & Schuster Children's Publishing, 2024.

ABOUT THE AUTHOR

MARK STEWART has written more than 150 non-fiction books for educational publishers, covering history, sports, and popular culture. His family tree tells a complex story common to many Americans. Mark's ancestors include some of the first European colonists, as well as the Indigenous people with whom early settlers interacted. Some faced off on the field of battle while others fought side-by-side. His 10th great-grandfather was **Myles Standish**, an officer on the *Mayflower*, while his ninth great-grandmother was **Singing Bird Corbison**, who was described as a "Shawnee woman" but who was probably from the **Wampanoag** tribe. The Wampanoag people saved Standish and his fellow **Pilgrims** from starvation during the winter of 1620–21, forming the basis for the story of Thanksgiving. The descendants of Corbison and Standish blended into a single family in 1789, and then headed west in search of opportunity. This brought Mark's ancestors into direct conflict with Native people along the frontier in the 1700s and 1800s. Mark's sixth great-grandmother recalled frantically casting bullets for her husband as they defended their small Kentucky fort from an attack. Another served under 23-year-old **Abraham Lincoln** in the Illinois Militia during the Black Hawk War of 1832. Mark's more recent ancestors chose to fight their battles with words—as writers and editors of books, newspapers, and magazines. In 2007, he authored a history of the **Indian Removal Act of 1830** and the infamous **Trail of Tears**.

INDEX